13311
Julie Krone: Fearless Jockey (Great
Comeback Champions)
Jim Spence
AR B.L.: 4.5
Points: 0.5   MG

GREAT COMEBACK CHAMPIONS

Julie
KRONE
Fearless Jockey

Written and Illustrated by Jim Spence

THE ROURKE PRESS, INC.
VERO BEACH, FL 32964

Edited by Sandra A. Robinson and Pamela J.P. Schroeder

LIBRARY OF CONGRESS CATALOGING-IN-PUBLICATION DATA

Spence, Jim.
    Julie Krone, fearless jockey / written and illustrated by Jim Spence.
       p. cm. — (Great comeback champions)
    ISBN 1-57103-007-7
    1. Krone, Julie—Juvenile literature. 2. Jockeys—United States—Biography—Juvenile literature. 3. Women jockeys—United States—Biography—Juvenile literature. [1. Krone, Julie. 2. Jockeys. 3. Women—Biography.] I. Title. II. Series: Spence, Jim. Great comeback champions.
SF336.K7S64 1995
798.4'0092—dc20
[B]   95-1006
                                        CIP
                                        AC

Printed in the USA

"Around the final turn and heading home, it's Consider the Lily!" the voice booms out of the loudspeaker at Belmont Park. "The winner by a length and a half is Consider the Lily!"

This is the story of the world's greatest female jockey—Julie Krone.

Growing Up

Julie Krone grew up on a horse farm in Eau Claire, Michigan. She was only two years old when her mother first put her on a horse. Right away, Julie fell in love with riding. Julie's mother was once a Michigan state champion rider. She wanted her daughter to learn the right way to ride.

Every morning, Julie and her mom woke up early
and practiced riding skills together. Then Julie
would have her breakfast, take a shower and catch
the bus for another day of school. With her mother's
help, Julie quickly became very good rider.

By the time she turned 13, Julie was an excellent rider. She had already won several horse shows, competing against riders twice her age.

When it came to riding, Julie was also quite a daredevil. Her favorite trick was to race straight for the barn riding bareback—standing up! When her head was just about to hit the barn, she would suddenly do the splits and land seated on her horse.

Julie had lots of fun doing tricks, but her real dream was to become a jockey.

Chasing Her Dream

At 15, Julie decided she was ready to chase her dream. She moved to Tampa, Florida, home of the Tampa Bay Downs racetrack, and lived with her grandparents. One day she went to the racetrack to apply for a job as a jockey. When the guard at the front gate would not let her in, Julie jumped the fence.

Once inside, Julie met a trainer named Jerry Pace. She began to show him photographs of her riding skills. Mr. Pace was impressed by this spunky kid, and decided he'd give her a try. Within five weeks, under his guidance, Julie Krone won her first race as a jockey!

Meeting a Friend

Julie worked the next several months as an apprentice, or student, jockey at Tampa Bay Downs. One day she went into one of the offices to fill out some papers. The secretary told Julie she had seen her race and began to offer some riding advice.

"What makes you so smart?" asked Julie. "Why, you're just a secretary."

Just then the woman rolled out from behind her desk in a wheelchair. Her name was Julie Snellings. She was once a very good jockey, until she fell during a race. The fall left her with her legs paralyzed—never able to race again. As they shook hands, neither guessed they would soon become best friends.

Julie Snellings liked Julie Krone and thought she had a talent. She found Julie an agent, who in turn helped Julie ride faster horses in bigger events. Helping her new friend, Julie Snellings began to feel important again. After her accident she got very lonely. Other jockeys avoided her, because they thought she was bad luck.

However, Julie Krone wasn't going to let any superstitions get in the way of their friendship. On August 25, four years to the day of Snellings' accident, Julie wore Snellings' old riding outfit and won three races at the Delaware Park Racetrack! Snellings was thrilled. "The 25th of August used to be such a sad day for me, but now Julie's made it my lucky day!"

Reaching the Top

Many of the jockeys did not like riding against Julie. They believed the sport of horse racing was no place for a young woman. However, in the years that followed, Julie showed the world what a great rider she was.

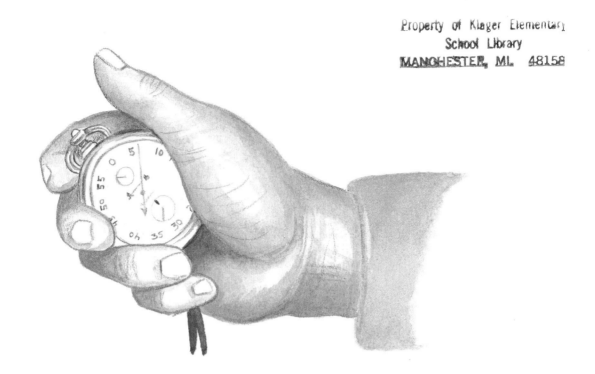

Julie Krone became the first woman to win a riding title at a major track, winning the Atlantic City riding title in 1982, and again in 1983. She was the first woman to win five races in one day, and was the leading money winner from 1987 through 1990, at both Monmouth and Meadowlands racetracks in New Jersey.

By 1987 Julie had become the number one female rider in the nation. She was famous, appearing on several TV shows. Julie Krone was even invited to the White House to meet the President of the United States!

On June 5, 1993, Julie Krone galloped straight into the record books. When she won the Belmont Stakes riding a horse named Colonial Affair, she became the first woman in history to capture a leg of the Triple Crown.

Fighting Back

On August 30, 1993, Julie had a terrible accident
at Saratoga Racetrack. Riding a horse named Seattle
Way, she came off the final turn and was ready to
make her move toward the finish line. Suddenly
another horse cut right in front of Julie's horse.

The legs of both horses tangled and they crashed!
Julie was thrown off her horse and lay helplessly on
the ground. Another rider tried to avoid her but it
was too late, Julie was trampled. Luckily for Julie,
the protective vest she was wearing saved her life.
She spent the next three weeks in a hospital bed.

Julie suffered many injuries from her accident. For nine months she was away from the sport she loved. During this time of recovery, she often became depressed, wondering if she would ever have the strength to race again.

Julie Krone was a fighter. On May 26, 1994, riding her favorite racehorse of all, Consider the Lily, Julie once again raced at New York's Belmont Park. As she raced toward the finish line the crowd began to shout, "Come on, Julie!" Julie Krone was back in saddle and the winner's circle again.

Today she is known throughout the world as the greatest female jockey of all time.

"After my accident, Julie was just the kind of person I needed around me," says Julie Snellings. "She has given me the courage to enjoy life again!"

Julie

KRONE

TIMELINE AND TRIUMPHS

1963	Born July 24, in Benton Harbor, Michigan
1981	First win, Tampa Bay Downs riding Lord Farkle
1982-83	Won Atlantic City riding title
1987	Number one female rider in the United States
1987-89	First woman to win riding title at a major track at Monmouth Park, New Jersey
1988-90	Won riding title at Meadowlands, New Jersey
1992	Led all riders at Belmont Park with 73 victories

1992   Earned over $9.2 million

1992   Ranked ninth-best jockey in the United
       States

1993   First woman to win Belmont Stakes
       Triple Crown

1993   Suffered terrible accident at Saratoga
       Racetrack

1994   Nine months after accident came back
       to win at Belmont Park, New York

1995   Won American Sportscasters
       Association Comeback Award

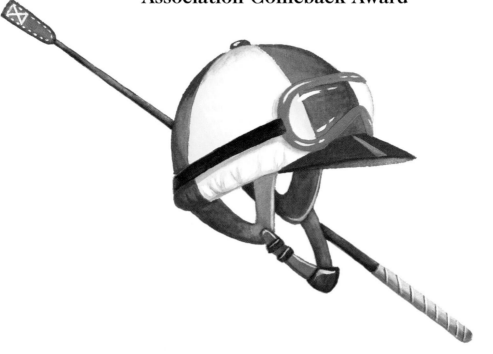

GREAT COMEBACK CHAMPIONS

ARTHUR ASHE
Tennis Legend

BO JACKSON
Super Athlete

JOE MONTANA
The Comeback Kid

JULIE KRONE
Fearless Jockey

MUHAMMAD ALI
The Greatest

NANCY KERRIGAN
Courageous Skater